OLD ENOUGH to MAKE a DIFFERENCE

Written by **Rebecca Hui**
Illustrated by **Anneli Bray**
Foreword by **Jonah Larson**

MAGIC CAT PUBLISHING

NEW YORK

Calling all social entrepreneurs!

Hello, I'm Jonah.

I taught myself to crochet when I was five years old. Since then, I have started a business called Jonah's Hands, which has a goal of bringing the world together, one stitch at a time.

My parents adopted me from Ethiopia when I was six months old, and I was given opportunities that my brothers and sisters in Ethiopia were not. So I decided to make a better world. I teamed up with Roots Ethiopia to build a library and a science center in the region where I was born, using the proceeds of my crocheted items.

The children in this book teach us that when each of us takes action, we can help resolve social problems or work to save the planet.

You don't have to wait until you are a grown-up to start making a social impact. You could do something close to home, or—as in my case—halfway around the globe.

The future of our world begins with you . . . today!

JONAH LARSON
Social entrepreneur and founder of Jonah's Hands

In this book, meet twelve
real-life children . . .

Maya from Georgia, USA

Fighting fast fashion

Lena from Germany

Working to end period poverty

Reyhan from Azerbaijan

Promoting green energy

Fabiënne from the Netherlands

Reducing paper waste

Aahan and Amal from the UK

Putting a stop to single-use straws

Archie from Australia

Ambassador of the Seabin Project

Chmba from Malawi

Supporting women and girls
through arts and education

Jiahua from China

Redistributing food destined
for landfills

Jefferson from Kenya

Growing food through
sustainable farming

Thomas from France

Protecting our oceans

Chaeli from South Africa

Campaigning for disability access

Omid from Italy

Making healthcare more accessible

End the trend of fast fashion . . .

Maya from Georgia was concerned about the environmental impact of "fast fashion"—when cheap clothes are made very quickly, only to be worn for a short time and thrown away.
So, at eight years old, she launched eco-fashion brand Maya's Ideas to sell clothes made from organic, recycled, and vintage materials. She also spends her time educating others about the impact that the fashion industry has on the planet.

Cheap clothes are often made by means that are harmful to the environment, such as the use of synthetic materials, like polyester and acrylic.

Globally, three out of five items of clothing end up on landfill sites within a year of purchase.

Maya's Ideas

NAME: Maya Penn
COUNTRY: USA
CHANGEMAKER FOR:
Reducing the
environmental
footprint of fashion

CREATE

Maya explains why it's important
to wear sustainable clothes.

DREAM BIG!

Fashion is one of the most environmentally
destructive industries in the world.

Around the world, huge quantities
of fresh water are used to dye
synthetic materials to make clothes.

When synthetic clothes are washed, they shed tiny
microplastic particles, which can travel to the ocean
and be swallowed by fish, making them sick.

Reduce paper waste . . .

Fabiënne from the Netherlands was roused to action after watching videos of forests being cut down all over the world. When she was seventeen years old, she started Grow a Wish and began to sell greeting cards made from recycled paper that contain a surprise inside: seeds! Instead of throwing the greeting card away, you can plant it and watch it grow into basil, tomatoes, or summer flowers to help the environment.

Fabiënne sells a greeting card that will grow into a beautiful plant.

Around the world, an estimated four billion trees are cut down every year to make paper products.

Many greeting cards can feature embellishments such as ribbons, glitter, or foil, which cannot be recycled.

We live in a throwaway culture—a society that uses products for a short time and then disposes of them.

Plants clean our water, soil, and air—making our environment a healthier place to live.

By growing your own garden, you can decide what goes into the soil, preventing harmful chemicals from polluting our environment.

NAME: Fabiënne Overbeek

COUNTRY: The Netherlands

CHANGEMAKER FOR: Creating greeting cards that can be planted rather than discarded

Say no to single-use plastic . . .

After seeing plastic straws littering the ocean while on holiday, British brothers Aahan, thirteen, and Amal, seventeen, decided to set up their own straw business, **The Last Straw Cheltenham.** They sell bamboo and wheat straws to stores, restaurants, and cafés as a sustainable alternative to single-use plastic straws. They also campaign to inform others of the devastating effects of plastic on the oceans.

Bamboo is the world's fastest-growing plant. It is an environmentally friendly alternative to plastic, as it is durable and compostable.

In most places, plastic straws cannot be recycled, and many end up in the oceans.

The best way to fight plastic is to avoid buying it in the first place.

Around the world, millions of plastic straws are used every day, and each one can take 200 years to biodegrade.

Amal hand-delivers bamboo and wheat straws to his local cafe.

Made from natural and organically grown wheat plant stems, wheat straws are fully compostable.

Aahan explains the impact of plastic straws on the oceans.

Bamboo

NAME: Aahan and Amal Patel
COUNTRY: UK
CHANGEMAKERS FOR: Eliminating single-use plastic straws

Prevent ocean pollution . . .

When twelve-year-old Archie learned about the importance of clean oceans, he decided to become a Seabin ambassador in Australia, where he lives. He campaigned for the installation of Seabins—floating trash bins that filter ocean plastic and debris—and partnered with local marinas who match the money Archie raises from his community. So far, Archie has installed three Seabins in Pittwater, New South Wales, Australia. His ultimate goal is to see the oceans free of trash.

CLEANER MARINA = CLEANER OCEANS

Archie installs a Seabin in his local marina.

Every minute, a garbage truck of plastic is dumped into our oceans.

Plastic can be broken into smaller pieces— known as microplastics—that can find their way into ocean food chains.

There are more microplastics in our oceans than there are stars in the Milky Way.

154

NAME: Archie Mandin
COUNTRY: Australia
CHANGEMAKER FOR:
Cleaning the oceans

Each Seabin moves up and down with the tide, collecting an average of 9.3 pounds of trash every day.

Seabins are located at marinas and ports, which are perfect locations to stop floating trash from entering the open ocean.

End period poverty . . .

Lena, from Germany, first traveled to Namibia when she was three years old. A little over a decade later, she returned and saw how important it is for children to have access to education. But without access to period products, many girls have to stay at home. So she set up an organization, Wadadee Cares, dedicated to keeping children in school. And one of its projects, NamPads, provides sustainable, reusable sanitary napkins made by local seamstresses.

Education is a basic human right for all.

Periods are a natural process and a part of many girls' lives.

$$1 + 1 = 2$$
$$2 + 2 = 4$$
$$3 + 3 =$$

Period poverty means being unable to access sanitary products due to their cost.

NAME: Lena Palm
COUNTRY: Germany
CHANGEMAKER FOR:
Providing sanitary
products to keep
girls in school

Lena hands fabric to
a local seamstress.

In the United Kingdom, an estimated
49 percent of girls have missed a day
of school due to their periods.

Share skills to help others . . .

When artist Chmba found out that girls whose families live in poverty are forced to leave school early, she developed a sustainable solution, even though she was only sixteen at the time. She launched Tiwale and trains women and girls to dye fabrics to sell in their home country of Malawi. The money made from sales provides grants for those interested in going back to school. So far, Chmba has helped over three hundred women and girls, with each individual keeping 60 percent of their profits and giving 40 percent back for the future training of others.

When young girls face barriers to education early in life, it is more difficult for them to get a job when they are older.

Around the world, nearly one in four girls between the ages of fifteen and nineteen are neither employed nor in school or training.

Globally, education increases earnings by up to 10 percent for each additional year in school.

Chmba teaches others to dye fabrics.

Women living in the world's poorest countries are less likely to get the education they need or bank the money they earn.

Equal rights and opportunities help everyone fulfill their potential.

TIWALE

TIWAL

TIWAL

Provide food to those in need...

When Jiahua learned that lots of food was being thrown away in her home country of China, she decided to make use of the food waste. At the age of seventeen, she set up PDT Food Depot to take food that would end up in landfills and give it to people in need. She has collected more than thirty tons of food from supermarkets, farms, and factories, and redistributed it to over forty communities so far.

Food that is fit for humans to eat but isn't eaten is called food waste. Food may be left to spoil or is thrown away because it has passed its use-by date or is no longer wanted.

Over one-third of all food produced is lost or wasted every year globally.

Jiahua helps a community member select their food for the week.

NAME: Jiahua Chen
COUNTRY: China
CHANGEMAKER FOR: Redistributing food destined for landfills

It takes a lot of energy and resources to produce, process, and transport food. When we throw it away, we're not only wasting the food, but also all the energy that's gone into making it.

When food waste ends up in landfills, it generates methane, a greenhouse gas that is harmful to the environment.

Some studies have shown that reducing food waste is the number one solution to the climate crisis.

Grow your own food . . .

Jefferson was six years old when he realized that food security was an issue for his community in his home country of Kenya. The local farms were hit by a drought that affected the crops, leaving his community hungry. Ten years later, he started a sustainable food system and grew hydroponic tomatoes indoors. His eco-friendly business, Eden Horticultural Hub, runs four hydroponics systems to supply tomatoes to more than a hundred households and lunches to fifteen hundred students.

A sustainable food system delivers food security and nutrition for all.

Food is a big contributor to climate change and global biodiversity loss because of the land and resources it uses.

Severe weather changes like droughts can destroy a farm's crops and lead to food insecurity for the community if it doesn't have reliable access to food.

Hydroponics allows a plant to grow in nutrient-rich water without soil.

Hydroponics provides an opportunity to predictably produce more food around the world using fewer natural resources.

Jefferson picks and packs a crop of tomatoes.

NAME: Jefferson Kang'acha
COUNTRY: Kenya
CHANGEMAKER FOR: Preventing hunger through sustainable food systems

Use green energy . . .

Reyhan was just fourteen years old when she designed a smart device for green energy that could generate electricity from raindrops. She came up with the idea in her home country of Azerbaijan. She thought that rather than rainwater disrupting their electrical supply, it could create it instead! Her invention fills a water tank with rainwater that flows at high speeds through an electric generator to produce energy. When there is no rain, the energy can still be stored in batteries. To promote her invention, Reyhan founded a company named Rainergy with the motto, "Light up one house at a time."

Green energy is any energy that is generated from natural resources, such as sunlight, wind, or water.

Reyhan monitors the collection of rainwater.

The Rainergy device eases pressure on local power grids by giving communities an extra source of electricity.

Green energy sources are naturally replenished, as opposed to fossil fuel sources, like natural gas or coal, which can take millions of years to develop.

When it rains, millions of gallons of water can fall, and the volume has enormous electric potential.

Green energy sources release less carbon dioxide into the atmosphere than natural gas or coal-based energy.

NAME: Reyhan Jamalova

COUNTRY: Azerbaijan

CHANGEMAKER FOR: Promoting green energy

Educate others to protect our oceans . . .

Fourteen-year-old Thomas from France knew how important it is to protect our oceans, so he set up a boat school to educate others. He sailed around the Atlantic Ocean, visiting schools to inform children about the harmful effects of acidification and overfishing. His organization, Children for the Oceans, is now a worldwide community of ambassadors who provide educational materials on ocean conservation.

The oceans are becoming more acidic because of the extra carbon dioxide in the atmosphere caused by humans cutting down forests and burning fossil fuels.

Overfishing is when people catch fish faster than they can be replenished. This can affect the ecosystem and disrupt the food chain.

At least 50 percent of the oxygen produced on Earth originates from marine plants that live in the oceans.

Thomas removes a fishing net from the water.

The acid in the oceans softens the shells of certain sea creatures and causes fish to lose their sense of smell.

Overfishing can lead to "bycatch," which is when sea creatures like turtles are accidentally caught in fishing nets.

NAME: Thomas Lesage
COUNTRY: France
CHANGEMAKER FOR:
Promoting ocean education

Champion a more inclusive world . . .

Diagnosed with cerebral palsy at eleven months old, Chaeli from South Africa has been a wheelchair user her whole life. At the age of nine, Chaeli, along with her sister and three friends, started a fundraiser to buy a motorized wheelchair to provide Chaeli with more freedom and independence. This fundraiser was the start of the Chaeli Campaign, a social justice organization cofounded to promote and provide the mobility and educational needs of children with disabilities.

Between 93 million and 150 million children live with a disabilities worldwide.

Chaeli explains how a motorized wheelchair gives her independence.

CHAELI CAMPAIGN

Children with disabilities are more likely to miss out on school than other children.

Children with disabilities may need to use equipment that can help them, such as a wheelchair or hearing aids.

NAME: Michaela "Chaeli" Mycroft
COUNTRY: South Africa
CHANGEMAKER FOR: Advancing inclusivity for children with disabilities

GOAL!

Every day, children with disabilities face barriers, such as accessibility, lack of support, or limited resources.

Children with disabilities can flourish in society and change negative attitudes about their abilities.

In some countries, people have access to healthcare whenever they need it, but for others, this is not an option.

Some people don't get the healthcare services they need because they don't have enough money or they live too far away from providers who offer them.

Having access to healthcare is a basic human right.

Build a community of caregivers . . .

When fifteen-year-old Omid's best friend lost his father due to heart failure, he decided to act. He founded Aid You (Mobile Cardiologist) in his home country of Italy, which provides affordable and accessible medical devices to monitor patients in need. The community-based initiative trains local volunteers in first-aid skills to help patients in times of emergencies. Omid also teamed up with a cofounder from Uganda to provide the same services throughout East Africa.

EVERY BEAT COUNTS

AIDU!

Access to healthcare impacts a person's quality of life.

Omid teaches a life-saving medical procedure.

Increasing access to healthcare services, like lowering costs or offering government support, can help more people get the care they need.

YOUR ECG

AID U!

NAME: Omid Gholamzadeh Nasrabadi

COUNTRY: Italy

CHANGEMAKER FOR: Making healthcare accessible to everyone

How can you help build a more sustainable world?

Addressing the social and environmental challenges facing our planet will require a generation of social innovators and changemakers. Social entrepreneurs are agents of positive change who address challenges through an enterprising approach. They develop businesses with a social or environmental purpose, reinvest profits into their mission, and are accountable for their actions. They combine insight, compassion, and imagination to create a better, fairer world.

1. Find your passion. Notice what is making you sad, angry, or excited, and transform that energy into creativity.

2. Tackle one problem at a time. Think about what you can do now—today. Think small, then dream big.

3. Have a clear social mission. Start simple first and let your values guide your journey.

4. Think global, act local. Even if your cause is a local one, look beyond to see what others have done around the world.

5. Keep prototyping. Try different things and do not be afraid to fail. Failure simply means there is something to be learned.

6. Do research. Learn more about the field you are interested in and who the key players are.

7. Involve others. A project grows when others can get involved, so engage with your community for help.

8. Stay up to date. Watch, listen, and read as much as you can to stay informed about the world around you.

9. Keep at it. Being entrepreneurial is hard work. Staying motivated and believing in yourself and your ideas is key.

10. Tell your story. Be confident and talk to your friends and family about why you're making a social impact.

Ten things you can do to be a responsible consumer:

1. Buy less. Before you decide to buy or not, ask yourself if you really need it. We can live without many things and we need less than we usually buy.

2. Choose quality over trends. Instead of buying trendy T-shirts that you'll wear once and need to replace, look for something timeless that's made to last.

3. Be selective. Opt for brands and shops that pride themselves on their quality and sustainable values.

4. Upcycle an old item. Instead of throwing something away, repair, decorate, or change it so that it can be used again as something more valuable.

5. Read and question labels. If a product is sustainable, it will always indicate this on the label. Also do your own research to make sure the product is not harmful to the environment.

6. Use green energy. Switch electrical items off when not in use, turn the heating down, and consider asking your family to change your energy provider to a greener alternative.

7. Avoid plastic packaging. Opt for reusable items, such as carrying your own reusable bag or water bottle.

8. Limit food waste. Keep track of the food you've bought to avoid throwing any away.

9. Consume seasonal produce. Buy seasonal fruits and vegetables, grown in local places, to avoid the promotion of intensive horticultural productions in other areas, which demand large amounts of water.

10. Be aware. No one can be a perfect consumer, but by becoming more aware of ethical practices, we can start to hold companies to higher standards.

Further reading

With the help of an adult, find out more about the children and issues featured in this book at their websites:

entrepreneurship-campus.org

globalcitizen.org

peacefirst.org

wearefamilyfoundation.org

mayasideas.com

growawish.nl

thelaststrawcheltenham.co.uk

seabinproject.com

wadadeecares.com

tiwale.org

childrenfortheoceans.eu

chaelicampaign.org

REBECCA HUI is an artist and social entrepreneur. She studied business administration at the University of California, Berkeley, and city planning, design, and development at MIT before starting Roots Studio, a company that reimagines cultural preservation by building bridges between rural communities and the global fashion market. Rebecca is driven by an ethos of sustainability, and is a Forbes 30 Under 30, Cartier Women's Initiative Laureate, and Echoing Green Fellow.

ANNELI BRAY is a children's illustrator from England. From an early age, she could be found painting stories about animals and magical creatures, making books about ponies, and reading voraciously. Anneli graduated with a degree in illustration from Norwich University of the Arts, became a bookseller (drawing on breaks), and at night dreamed of having her own illustrations in a book one day. Now she is best known for her warm, colorful illustrations that is influenced by her love of travel, nature, and adventure.

JONAH LARSON is a crochet prodigy from Wisconsin. Jonah began crocheting at five years old and has been making a social impact ever since. He donates his crocheting proceeds and has built a library and science center in the village in Ethiopia from where he was adopted. Jonah also runs his own business, Jonah's Hands, which features his crochet tutorials. Jonah was named a Young Entrepreneur of the Year in his home state, and his infectious desire to give back has earned him a worldwide following.

The illustrations in this book were created using gouache, colored pencils, and digital media.
Set in Rainer and Panforte Pro.

Library of Congress Control Number 2022934431
ISBN 978-1-4197-6599-5

Text © 2022 Rebecca Hui • Foreword by Jonah Lawson
Illustrations © 2022 Anneli Bray
Cover © 2022 Magic Cat
Book design by Nicola Price

Printed and bound in China
10 9 8 7 6 5 4 3 2 1

ABRAMS The Art of Books
195 Broadway, New York, NY 10007
abramsbooks.com